# Zeek
## The Christmas Tree Mouse

To Betts

# Zeek
## The Christmas Tree Mouse

RICHARD H. SCHNEIDER

ILLUSTRATED BY

FLORENCE S. DAVIS

Abingdon Press
*Nashville*

ZEEK, THE CHRISTMAS TREE MOUSE

Copyright © 2002 by Abingdon Press

All rights reserved.
No part of this work may be reproduced or transmitted in any form or by any means, electronic or mechanical, including photocopying and recording, or by any information storage or retrieval system, except as may be expressly permitted by the 1976 Copyright Act or in writing from the publisher. Requests for permission should be addressed in writing to Abingdon Press, Permissions Office, 201 Eighth Avenue South, P. O. Box 801, Nashville, TN 37202-0801.

Library of Congress Cataloging-in-Publication Data for ZEEK, THE CHRISTMAS TREE MOUSE is available from the Library of Congress.

02 03 04 05 06 07 08 09 10 11—10 9 8 7 6 5 4 3 2

PRINTED IN HONG KONG

Zeek pressed his little gray ear to the floor above him.

"Mother, what's going on up there?"

Mother Mouse turned from the big piece of cheese to her son. "Oh, every year at this time the people up there have a big celebration. It goes on for days, but it all seems to become very important on one special night."

"What do they celebrate?" asked Zeek. "Did they find a nice piece of cheese like we have?"

Mother Mouse handed a morsel to Zeek's little sister, called Sister Dear. "I don't know, son," she said, "but one year through a crack in the wall I saw a tree growing in their living room. It wasn't like any tree I had seen before. At first I thought it was on fire. There were bright burning things all over it. Beautiful shiny objects hung from its branches. But just then that terrible cat came scratching at the wall and I hurried out of there."

"**H**mmmm," said Zeek, listening to the hubbub above.

"Now don't get any ideas about going up there," said Mother Mouse sharply. "We are lucky to live off the crumbs that fall to the floor. And once in a while," she smiled, her paw patting the cheese, "we find a feast."

But Zeek wasn't listening to his mother. He was thinking about all the wonderful things going on above him. Besides, he was a very smart mouse, smarter than his mother knew, or so he thought.

Soon Mother Mouse and Sister Dear were sound asleep in their warm bed of cotton yarn and wool scraps. But Zeek couldn't sleep. He lay awake, his shining eyes staring curiously at the floor above him. He noticed that it had become very quiet.

He pushed his wool scrap away and, careful not to awaken his mother and sister, crept to their doorway to the big people's house. The door was really a hole in the kitchen baseboard under the stove. Zeek was very careful, for he remembered the terrible time when his father did not come home. His mother cried and cried. That's when she warned him and his sister about the cat.

"Never, never go up there until you are big enough to run very fast … very fast," she said, brushing a tear from her dark eyes.

**B**ut surely, he thought, everyone, including the cat, must be asleep. Besides, he was a very fast mouse and it was so quiet. Zeek slipped out under the stove and peered into the living room, his whiskers quivering.

What was that strange light? Quietly he crept closer, then caught his breath. It was the most amazing thing he had ever seen. A big tree growing in the corner of the room ablaze with many colors. He blinked in fascination.

Suddenly, a sound! He turned, his heart stopping. It was snoring, like his mother made after a long, hard day gathering crumbs. Only it was much gruffer and louder. He looked over to the chair from which the sound came.

There was the cat. Sound asleep.

**Z**eek sighed in relief.

As long as he stayed very, very quiet, he would learn more about this strange tree. He crept closer to its trunk, which was planted in a big red metal bucket. He looked up; the tree smelled so good. And all those wonderful things hanging from its branches, shining objects of red, silver, blue, and gold. And in such strange shapes.

Then he saw it. A gingerbread man way up in the tree. His mouth watered. He had tasted a piece of gingerbread man once. While the big people were baking, one of the gingerbread men had fallen to the floor and broken. Mother had triumphantly carried a piece home. Oh, how he had loved its spicy flavor!

**H**e looked up at the gingerbread man slowly turning on its string. Could he? He remembered his mother's warning. But, oh, he also remembered that wonderful taste. Licking his little lips, he decided he would.

Carefully, he climbed up into the tree, from branch to branch, higher and higher, breaking off pine needles which pattered to the snowy skirt on the floor below. Closer and closer he approached his prize. Soon he was right next to the gingerbread man. With a thumping heart, he leaned over … and bit off its foot.

Ugh! Zeek spat the piece out and wrinkled his nose. It didn't taste at all like the gingerbread man Mother brought home. It tasted like the plaster he once nibbled from the wall.

Zeek shuddered and backed into a glass ball ornament behind him. It tumbled noisily down into the tree, leaving only its string hooked to a branch. Terrified, he looked down at the cat. But he was still snoring in front of the fire. Zeek breathed a sigh of relief.

At that very moment, the front door opened and all the big people came trooping in, talking excitedly. He heard sentences like, "Wasn't that a lovely Christmas Eve service?" and "Don't you like to sing all the verses to 'Silent Night'?"

Zeek couldn't run down the tree and escape. They would see him. Besides, the cat was awake, stretching!

Oh, what could he do?

Suddenly he had an idea.

He would become a tree ornament, just like the others. He snatched a little red cap from a plastic Santa near him, pulled it over his head, grabbed the fallen ornament's empty string with his right paw, and hung on. He fixed a big smile on his face as the children rushed up to the tree.

"Isn't it beautiful … the best we ever had!"

And then one of them said, "Where did we get that mouse ornament? Isn't he cute?"

Zeek hung as still as he could. He could feel mouse sweat under his Santa cap.

One little girl pressed her finger into his round tummy.

"Oh," she squealed, "he feels soft, just like a beanbag toy!"

**A**t her touch, Zeek started slowly spinning around and around. He was getting dizzy, but forced himself to keep smiling. He looked down and saw the cat watching him.

The cat knew!

It licked its chops with its long pink tongue.

Zeek's arm was getting so tired and his face ached from the put-on smile. Oh, what a terrible fix he had gotten himself into. All for a bit of awful plaster.

He saw the children settle down at their father's feet. The man opened a big book and began reading. It was about a father and mother-to-be journeying to a town called Bethlehem.

**Z**eek was so tired. His aching arm felt like it was on fire. He wanted to cry. But he couldn't help but listen as the man told about a little baby being born and shepherds and animals coming to worship him. When the man closed the book, he told the children about someone called God who had sent the baby.

"Is it true that God created the earth and every living thing?" asked a child.

"Yes," answered the father.

"Like our cat?" asked another.

"And the mice who live under the floor?"

"Yes," said the father, "even the mice."

"Do they pray to God," piped one, "and ask for God's help when they need it?"

The father smiled. "I don't know," he said. "But it's late now and we must all get to bed. You know we will be getting up early tomorrow to open presents."

The family filed out and Zeek wondered if this was his chance to escape. But the cat remained behind, looking up at him, showing his big white teeth.

*Oh … oh*, sighed Zeek, *I can't hold on another minute. My arm is about to break in two. What can I do?*

Big tears slid down his furry cheeks and dropped off his whiskers to plop onto the book the father had left below the tree. Zeek thought about the One called God who had created him and who answered prayers. Could he pray too?

Hanging on with all his might, Zeek softly sobbed, "Oh, God, please forgive me. I know I have been bad. I disobeyed my mother. But I am just a poor little mouse and you are the only one who can save me."

Zeek barely breathed those last words, knowing he would soon drop—right into the jaws of the cat below. But when he looked down, the cat was gone!

What? Where? Then Zeek heard the snoring. The cat had settled in front of the fireplace and was fast asleep!

Zeek scampered down the tree, raced across the living room, into the kitchen, and through the door to his home where he quickly climbed into bed. But before going to sleep, he folded his little gray paws the way he had seen the children do and thanked God for saving him.

But Zeek wasn't out of trouble yet. The next morning he would have some explaining to do.

**B**ut Zeek wasn't out of trouble yet. The next morning he would have some explaining to do.